KEEP CATS AND CARRY ON

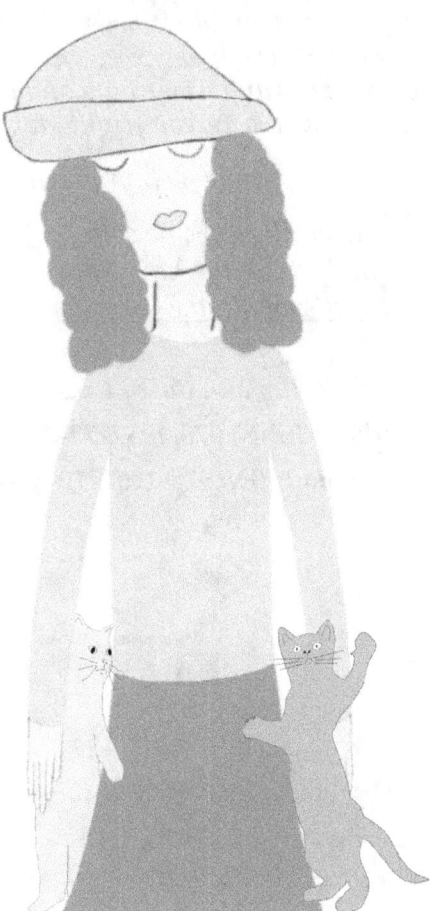

Keep Cats and Carry On
With Illustrations by Blythe Ayne
Quotes by Blythe Ayne and Others

Emerson & Tilman, Publishers
129 Pendleton Way #55
Washougal, WA 98671

www.BlytheAyne.com
Blythe@BlytheAyne.com
https://shop.BlytheAyne.com

Keep Calm and Carry Cats
Paperback ISBN: 978-1957272-82-5
Hard Bound ISBN: 978-1957272-83-2

KEEP
CATS
AND
CARRY
ON

"If you want to write, keep cats."

Aldous Huxley

Do Your Doodle!

_____

_____

_____

_____

_____

_____

_____

_____

_____

_____

_____

_____

_____

_____

_____

_____

_____

_____

_____

_____

_____

_____

"Time spent with cats is never wasted."

May Sarton

Let the Doodling Commence!

"A cat can purr its way out of anything."
Donna McCrohan

Doodle Here!

> "One small cat changes coming home to an empty house
> To coming home."
>
> *Pam Brown*

Time to Doodle!

"A cat allows you to sleep on the bed.
On the edge."

Jenny de Vries

Doodly-Doodly Doo!

"Cats are deep, deep wells
you throw your emotions into."
Bruce Schimmel

You Doodle! I Doodle!
Everybody Doodle!

"Have a kitten's enthusiasm for life!"

Blythe Ayne

Happy Doodle Day!

"Cats are a mysterious kind of folk."

Sir Walter Scott

May All Your Doodle Wishes Come True!

"What greater gift than the love of a cat?"

Charles Dickens

The World's Most Fun Doodles!

"The wise revere the wisdom of cats."

Blythe Ayne

Happy Heart Doodle!

Books & Audiobooks by Blythe Ayne

Joy Forest Cozy Mysteries:
A Loveliness of Ladybugs
A Haras of Horses
A Clowder of Cats
A Gaggle of Geese
A Round of Robins – the Novella
A Round of Robins – the Novel

The Darling Undesirables Series:
The Heart of Leo - novelette prequel
The Darling Undesirables
Moons Rising
The Inventor's Clone
Heart's Quest

Women's Paranormal Romance Novel:
Eos –The Log, Dark Road of Horse and Human

YA Series – The City Under Seattle
With Thea Thomas:
The People in the Mirror
Millie in the Mirror
The Angel in the Mirror

Middle Grade Novel:
Matthew's Forest

Children's Illustrated Books:
The Rat Who Didn't Like Rats
The Rat Who Didn't Like Christmas

Novellas & Short Story Collections:
5 Minute Stories
13 Lovely Frights for Lonely Nights
When Fields Hum & Glow

Nonfiction:
How to Save Your Life Series:
Save Your Life with the Dynamic Duo – D3 and K2
Save Your Life with Awesome Apple Cider Vinegar
Save Your Life With The Power Of pH Balance
Save Your Life With The Phenomenal Lemon
Save Your Life with Basic Baking Soda
Save Your Life with Stupendous Spices
Save Your Life with the Elixir of Water

Absolute Beginner Series:
Chair Yoga – Easy, Healing, Yoga Moves You Can Do with a Chair
Bed Yoga – Easy, Healing, Yoga Moves You Can Do in Bed
Bed Yoga for Couples—Easy, Healing, Yoga Moves You Can Do in Bed
Write Your Book! Publish Your Book! Market Your Book!

www.ingramcontent.com/pod-product-compliance
Lightning Source LLC
Chambersburg PA
CBHW071024120626
46546CB00003B/1207

* 9 7 8 1 9 5 7 2 7 2 8 2 5 *